Python

for

Beginners

The Absolute Beginners Guide to Python
Programming, Data Science and Predictive Model.

A Practical Introduction to Object Oriented
Programming Language.

(Essentials Cookbook)

Django Smith

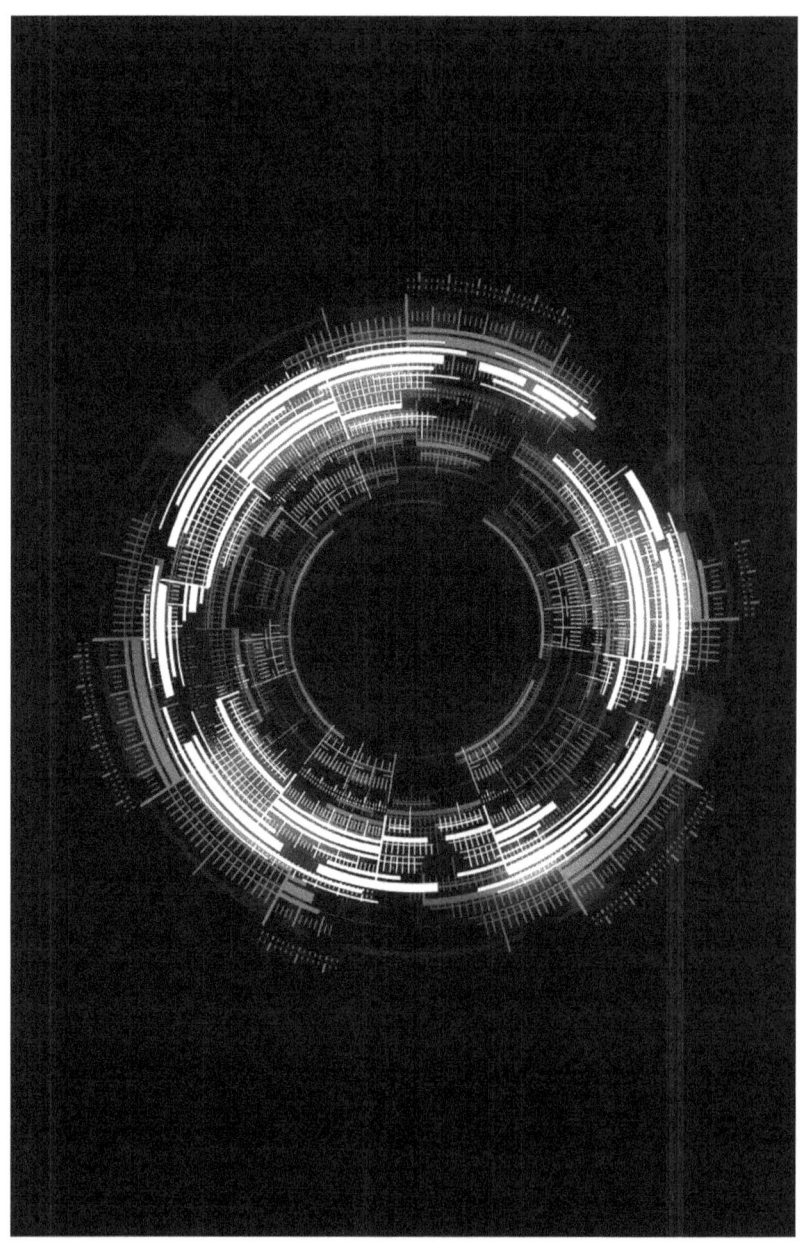

Table of Contents

liable for any hardship or damages that may befall them after undertaking information described herein.

Additionally, the information in the following pages is intended only for informational purposes and should thus be thought of as universal. As befitting its nature, it is presented without assurance regarding its prolonged validity or interim quality. Trademarks that are mentioned are done without written consent and can in no way be considered an endorsement from the trademark holder.

Introduction

Congratulations on purchasing *Python for Beginners* and thank you for doing so.

The following chapters will discuss everything that you need to know in order to get started with the Python coding language. There are a lot of different coding languages that you are able to work with, but none are going to give you the benefits, as well as ease of use, that you're going to find when you start with the Python coding language. This guidebook is going to spend some time looking at the steps that you need to take to get started with writing your very own codes, even if you are a beginner and have never done any coding in your life.

This guidebook is going to start out with some of the basics that come with the Python coding language. We will look at what the Python language is all about along with some of the benefits of using it, how to install this language, and some of the basic parts that come with your code. We will then move on to some of the different things you can do to get your feet wet with writing the codes that you want, including what the classes and objects are all about, how to work with the exceptions, and what those conditional statements are all about.

From there, we have so much more than we need to learn how to do with this kind of coding language, and this guidebook will make sure that you know how to make it happen. We will continue on looking at how to create lists and loops, the importance of Python files, how to do the functions in Python, data visualization, how to test your code, and where the regular expressions are able to come into the mix as well.

As you can see, there are a lot of different things that you are going to be able to do when you decide to work with the Python coding language. When you are ready to start learning how to do some of your own codes, and you want to be able to work on your own programs as soon as possible, make sure to check out this guidebook to help you get started.

There are plenty of books on this subject on the market, thanks again for choosing this one! Every effort was made to ensure it is full of as much useful information as possible. Please enjoy!

Chapter 1: What is the Python Language?

As you spend a little bit of time doing some research, you will find that there are actually a ton of different coding languages that you can work with. Some are going to be more advanced; some are designed to work the best online, and some just go with one operating system or another. Each of these is going to come with their own benefits and negatives, and choosing the one that you want to go with can be a challenge, especially if you have never worked with any kind of coding or computer language in the past.

Even with all of the different options out there, you may find that working with the Python coding language is going to be one of the best choices to help you out. It is a simple coding language, one that is going to help you to do some high and powerful things at the same time, without being a challenge for a beginner. In fact, this is often the coding language that is recommended for those who are just starting out with coding for the first time and who may not be familiar with what they should do to make this work for them.

There are a lot of things to love about this kind of language. It is easy to work with and learn, even with all of the power that comes with it. You will be able to write codes in no time and the wording is in English, unlike some of the other options you can choose out there, which makes it a bit easier to work with overall. And the other tools, like having some good libraries, help from many other people in the coding world, open source programming that is free and more makes it the perfect option when you are first getting started with this kind of language.

You will find that there are a lot of benefits that come with the Python language. The first benefit that we are going to take a look at is the support libraries. You will find that just by opening up the Python language, there are a lot of options available in the library. And you can look at third-party libraries and extensions that can easily be added to this coding language.

This is a great option for you, whether you are a beginner or more advanced with your coding. It is going to provide you with a lot of options on what you are able to do with your coding and can make things easier. You will be able to add in a lot of classes, objects, and functions in this, and that can make life so much easier overall. You can always work just with the libraries and extensions that come with the Python language when you download it, or you can go through and add in some third-party libraries to this if you would like some special features and more to work on your codes.

Integration features: Python can be great because it integrates what is known as the Enterprise Application Integration. This really helps with a lot of the different things you want to work on in Python including COBRA, COM, and more. It also has some powerful control capabilities as it calls directly through Java, C++, and C. Python also has the ability to process XML and other markup languages because it can run all of the modern operating systems, including Windows, Mac OS X, and Linux through the same kind of byte code.

More productivity for the programmer: The Python language has a lot of designs that are object-oriented and a lot of support libraries. Because of all these resources and how easy it is to use the program; the programmer is going to increase their productivity. This can even be used to help improve the productivity of the programmer while using languages like C#, C++, C, Perl, VB, and even Java.

Another benefit that you are going to enjoy when you get started with the Python language is that it is really easy to learn, while also being easily adaptable for a beginner when they are trying to figure things out. This guidebook is going to help you with this because we will discuss some of the basics that come with Python. And when you are done, you will be prepared to write out some of your own codes, ones that are powerful and strong, and you can even do your own projects.

Python is going to be an easy language for you to read through. As we work through the different things that you are able to do with Python in this guidebook, you will find that most of these codes, even though they do go through some powerful things to make your codes work, are going to be easy to read. There isn't going to be a ton of extras in the code with things that are impossible to understand. And you will quickly be able to learn how to read through a few of these codes on your own.

Before we move on too much, go through and look through a few of the codes that we have listed in this guidebook. Are you surprised by how easy it is to catch some of the words and maybe, with a little bit of translating, figure out what they are trying to do? Even if you don't fully understand what is going on in the code all of the time, at least the words are in English, and that can put your mind at ease about what is going on.

Even with this simplicity, and the fact that a lot of beginners like to go straight to this kind of language for their needs, you will find that the Python coding language is going to have a ton of power that goes with it. In fact, there are many people, even those who have worked with other coding languages in the past, who are surprised by the amount of power they are able to get with this kind of language. Even though you will often hear of Python being a beginner's language, you are able to adapt it and use it with many different programs and other languages that you would like to work on. It is possible to combine it with one or more other coding languages, ensuring that your program gets exactly what it needs.

Many people enjoy that there is a huge and active community that comes with this kind of coding language. Python, due to all of the benefits that we have talked about above, is one of the most popular of all the coding languages throughout the world. This community is going to be so useful to you as a beginner when it comes to learning more about the programs and the codes and will help you to get things down quickly. You can spend time reading through the community, watching the tutorials, and asking for help any time that the program isn't doing what you think it should. Before you get started with this, you can take some time to look at the community of Python to make sure that the codes are going to be as easy to work with as possible.

And the final benefit that we are going to take a look at is that this program is open sourced. This means that you won't have to worry about the code getting ruined by someone who just wants a lot of money. The original version of Python and the variations that are made off of it are free, and anyone is able to download it and make some adjustments to make it better and improve it over time. this will ensure that you are able to do what you want with this coding language, and get the results that you would like.

This means that when you are ready to work with the Python coding language, you will be able to do it for free. You can set up the Python program, and all of the interpreters and more than you need for free if you choose. Of course, there are some companies and individuals who will develop these a bit differently, or work with some special libraries and extensions that are special, and you will need to pay for those if you would like to work with them. But you do not have to purchase a single thing, in order to get the programming language up and running on your computer.

As you can see, there are a lot of things that you are going to be able to enjoy when it comes to working with the Python coding language. And all of these are reasons why many programmers, those who are new to the whole idea and those who have been around for a long time, are going to decide to learn this language. Make sure to check out the benefits above and see which one is the main reason why you want to be able to learn this kind of language for your own coding needs.

Python as an object-oriented programing language

Before we go too far into the idea of doing some coding and downloading the program with Python, you will need to take a few moments in order to learn more about OOP or object-oriented programming. If you have spent some time researching about Python in the past, these words may be something that you have heard about in the past, but you may not know what they all mean.

To help us get started with this, when you start to work with an OOP language, you will find that any of the coding's that you are doing is going to be so much easier compared to some of the older and more traditional coding languages. With an OOP language, you are working with a type that is going to classify your objects and classes in a way that is easy to work with and manipulate. You will see how this works a bit more when we look specifically at classes, but it basically means that it will be easier to organize the code that you are trying to write.

One of the features that you are going to enjoy using when you work with an OOP language is that the procedures of any object you use are going to have some power in them to access fields of data and even make some modifications to them. With this kind of language, you are able to design the program in the way that you want just by building it up from a series of objects that are going to talk and interact with one another.

This seems pretty simplistic, and if you have been worried about starting a coding language because of the challenge's others warn you about, you may feel that you are missing something. Or, you may be worried that the Python language doesn't have the power that you are looking for in a coding language for your specific program and that you need to look somewhere else.

But this is contrary to the truth. OOP languages are actually really diverse. Each language is going to have some differences, but the ones that you may use, including Python, are class based. This means that the code is going to have each of the objects belong to a class, which can help you keep things organized and allows you to know which object you will need to use.

As you work through Python, you will quickly find that an OOP language can make programming and code writing easier. If you ever spent time working with some of the older coding languages, you will notice that those older ones are much harder to work with and that OOP can make things easier. With the older coding languages, it's possible for your objects and other parts of the code to move around or end up in a different location than you had meant, which can make it hard to write the code and even debug it. But with an OOP language, you won't run into this problem because of the way that things are organized.

There are a lot of features that you are going to be able to find when you work with an OOP language. These are going to rely on classes, for the most part, to work well. These are going to also include a few other techniques and structures that you need to learn a little bit more about in order to get the results that you would like. Some of the features that are most likely to show up on this kind of language and help you to get things done include:

- Shared features from non-OOP languages: These languages may still have some features of low-level features from some of the older coding languages. Some of the examples of the features that are often still available in OOP languages include:
  - Variables: These variables are able to store your formatted information inside a few different data types. These are built-in to your languages such as integers and characters. Variables can include things like hash tables, string, and lists.
  - Procedures: These can go by different names such as subroutines, routines, functions, and

method. They are going to take your input and then generate an output that you can then use for manipulating your data. The newer languages will have more structured concepts like loops and conditionals, which are both used a lot in Python.

- Objects and classes, we will talk about these in a bit in more detail, but many times when you bring up an OOP language, you are going to see a lot about the classes. These classes, to keep things simple for now, are going to be the containers that you use to hold onto and store your objects, regardless of what types of objects you are exploring. This makes it easier to bring up those objects when it is needed.

- Encapsulation: You will find that when you work with an OOP language, you are going to also have a process that is known as encapsulation to help you. This is the process that has to come into place to bind data together. Any of the functions that are used for this kind of process are important because they are going to manipulate the data and ensure that it is secure from misuse within that code.

- Dynamic dispatch and passing of messages. As you work to write some of your codes, you will find that there could be some external codes, but these are not going to be the ones in charge of selecting the procedural code when it is time to execute. This is something that is going to be passed over to the object. The object is going to do this by looking at the method that is associated with that object during run time in a process that is known as dynamic dispatch.

- Open recursion: As you work through this OOP language, you may notice that it works with the idea of open recursion. This is basically when the object method is going to find itself called over with another method. You just need to use the keywords of this and self to help the process get going. These are going to be variables called late-bound, which means that they are going to let the method that has been defined in the class at hand invoke a method that you have placed in another class, or that you will define later on.

As you can see here, there are a lot of things that you are able to love when you decide to work with an OOP language. As you work through more of the different parts that come with the Python language in this guidebook, you are quickly going to see how great having an OOP language an be for learning and executing your own codes.

Chapter 2: Installing the Python Language

Now that we know a bit more about the Python language and why it is such a great tool to work with, it is time to move on and look at some of the steps that you need to take in order to get this installed on your computer. You want to make sure that you are able to go through and install this program in the proper way and to make sure that the right version is on your computer at the right time. this will make it easier to write some of the codes that you need, without too many struggles along the way.

Before any programmer is able to look at the other parts of this guidebook and start writing out their own codes with the Python language, it is important to go through and install the interpreter. Installation for Python is going to be depending on the kind of operating system that is on your computer, along with the source of installation that you decide to work with. There are going to be a few places where you are able to source this coding language, but we are going to focus on getting the information from www.python.org to make it easier.

In this chapter, we are going to take some time to look at the different steps that you have to use in order to install the

Python interpreter and more on all of the major operating systems. Go and look for the one that fits with the operating system that is on your computer, and then follow these steps in order to see the results that you want and to get the Python coding language, and everything that goes with it, installed on your computer.

Working with the Mac OS X

If you are using a Mac operating system when you want to install this, you will find that the Python 2 version is going to be there already, without having to go through and do anything else. The exact version of Python 2 that is on your computer is going to depend on how old the computer is and the version of the operating system that you have. If you would like to see which version of Python is on your computer at this time, open up your command prompt and type in "python – V"

This is going to show you the version number of Python that you have on your Mac operating system at this time.

Now, it is also possible for you to change up the version of Python that you would like to use. Many people like to work with the newest option of Python, Python 3, and this means that you will need to go through a few steps in order to get it all set up. You do not need to go through and uninstall the Python

2 version that you have in order to make this happen. To check if there is any Python 3 installation on your system, you need to open up the terminal app that we were using before and then type in "python3 – V" to check

The default that you will see with this kind of system is that Python 3 is not going to be installed on the computer at all like we just talked about. If you want to use Python 3 on this kind of computer system, you will need to visit that www.python.org that we talked about before and use the installers that are there. This is a good place to start with because it ensures that all of the things that you need for coding are going to be installed at the same time. This includes the Python shell, the interpreter, any tools that you need, and the IDLE.

Being able to run the IDLE and the shell with this language is going to depend on the version of this that you choose to work with and some of your own preferences when it comes to doing the code. The two commands that you will need to use in order to help you start up the IDLE and the shells application, depending on the version of Python that you would like to work with, include:

- For Python 2.X just type in "Idle"
- For Python 3.X, just type in "idle3"

As we talked about a bit before, when you take the time to download and install this Python 3 on the Mac operating system, you will need to install the IDLE so make sure that is there, and you can install it as a standard application inside of your Applications folder of course. To help you to start up this program using your desktop, you just need to go into the folder, double click on the application for the IDLE, and then you can wait for it to download.

Working with the Windows System

Now that we are all done with the Mac operating system, it is time to work with the Windows System. You may want to work with adding the Python on your computer. Windows is going to have its own programing language already on it, so you have to go through a few steps to manually add on Python in order to use it. This isn't going to be too hard for you to work with, but you need to take it to step by step and ensure that you don't rush through things to make it happen.

Python is going to work just fine when you are on a Windows computer. You just need to take the time to install it on the Windows operating system. But once it is all set up, the Python language is going to be easy to use on this kind of operating system, so you don't need to worry about that.

When you are ready to work with this language on the Windows operating system, you will need to go through and come up with the right variables for the environment that are needed to run the scripts for Python from the command prompt. Some of the steps that you need to take in order to work with Python on a Windows System include:

1. To set this up, you need to visit the official Python download page and grab the Windows installer. You can choose to do the latest version of Python 3, or go with another option. By default, the installer is going to provide you with the 32-bit version of Python, but you can choose to switch this to the 64-bit version if you wish. The 32-bit is often best to make sure that there aren't any compatibility issues with the older packages, but you can experiment if you wish.

2. Now right click on the installer and select "Run as Administrator." There are going to be two options to choose from. You will want to pick out "Customize Installation"

3. On the following screen, make sure all of the boxes under "Optional Features" are clicked and then click to move on.

4. While under "Advanced Options," you should pick out the location where you want Python to be installed.

Click on Install. Give it some time to finish and then close the installer.

5. Next, set the PATH variable for the system so that it includes directories that will include packages and other components that you will need later. To do this, use the following instructions:

   a. Open up the Control Panel. Do this by clicking on the taskbar and typing in Control Panel. Click on the icon.

   b. Inside the Control Panel, search for Environment. Then click on Edit the System Environment Variables. From here, you can click on the button for Environment Variables.

   c. Go to the section for User Variables. You can either edit the PATH variable that is there, or you can create one.

   d. If there isn't a variable for PATH on the system, then create one by clicking on New. Make the name for the PATH variable and add in the directories that you want. Click on close all the control Panel dialogs and move on.

6. Now you can open up your command prompt. Do this by clicking on Start Menu, then Windows System, and then Command Prompt. Type in "python." This is going to load up the Python interpreter for you.

Once you get through these steps (they are quicker than they seem), you will be able to open up the Python language and then use it the way that you would like on your Windows system. You can choose to get the interpreter and more set up the way that you need, and then write out the codes that you want and make the programs that you want.

Working with the Linux operating system.

The next operating system that we are going to look at is the Linux operating system. This is a big operating system that can work along with a lot of different systems, and this means that you need to spend some time making sure that you are learning to set up the Python coding language on this system as well. Let's take a look at some of the things that you can do to work on the Linux operating system and get Python set up on it.

The first thing to do here is to see if there is a version of Python 3 already on your system.

You can open up the command prompt on Linux and then run the following code:

```
$ python3 - - version
```

If you are on Ubuntu 16.10 or newer, then it is a simple process to install Python 3.6. you just need to use the following commands:

```
$ sudo apt-get update
$ sudo apt-get install Python3.6
```

If you are relying on an older version or Ubuntu or another version, then you may want to work with the deadsnakes PPA, or another tool, to help you download the Python 3.6 version. The code that you need to do this includes:

```
$ sudo apt-get install software-properties-common
$ sudo add-apt repository ppa:deadsnakes/ppa
# suoda apt-get update
$ sudo apt-get install python3.6
```

The good news that comes with this is that if you are working with the other distributions of Linux, it is very possible that you are going to have Python 3 that is on the system. If it is not there, you can use the distributions package manager to make this happen. And if you don't like the version of Python 3 is not recent enough, or you would like a different version, then you are able to go through and use the same steps to install a more recent version, or a different version, on the system as you would like to use.

Understanding the Python Interpreter

The next thing that we need to focus on a bit here is the Python interpreter. The standard installation of this coding language that you are able to get from www.python.org, is going to contain everything that you need to get this language started. it is going to contain documentation, information on licensing, and the files that are needed to run any of the scripts that you need to run any Python code. These three files are going to include the shell, the interpreter and the IDLE.

First, we need to take a look at the Python interpreter. This is going to be important because it is going to the part that will execute the codes that you decide to write in it. The interpreter is able to take the codes that you write and turns them into instructions. It will then process these in order to execute what you would like to see on the screen.

Then we need to work on the Python IDLE. This is known as the integrated development and learning environment. It is responsible for holding onto all of the different tools that are needed when you would like to create some programs with Python. You will find inside of this IDLE all of the tools that you need to debug the code, the text editor, and even the shell. Depending on which of the Python versions you would like to use, you can have a basic IDLE, or you can work with one that is more extensive.

There is a version of the IDLE that will come with the downloaded Python, but there are also some third-party ones that you can choose as well. You can find a new text editor and an IDLE to fit your needs a bit more, but the basic one that comes with your Python download is going to be just fine if you don't feel like changing it out.

And finally, we need to spend some time with the Python Shell. This is going to be an interactive command line driving interface that you will be able to find inside of the interpreter. This one is going to be responsible for holding onto the commands that you go through and write out. from there, it is going to go through and execute all of the code that you plan to write out. Any time that you find the code isn't understandable, then this means that you will get an error message and will need to go through and fix the issue.

Each of these three parts of the code is going to be super important when it comes to writing out the codes that you want to use. When you are working with the www.python.org installation, then all three of these points are going to be installed, and you won't need to do any more work to see it happen. If you get your Python downloaded from somewhere other than that website, then you need to double check the files and figure out if you need to download those three components on their own to get the code to work.

Chapter 3: The Basic Parts of Your Code

At this point, we have taken a bit of time to learn about the Python code and why it is such a great one to work with for your coding needs. Then we moved on to the steps that you need to take in order to get this code on your computer and set up to write your codes. And now it is time to actually look at some of the different parts that are going to come inside of your codes, ensuring that you are going to really be ready to go when we move on to some of the other topics in a bit.

After you have spent some time working with the Python language, it is likely that you will start to notice that a few different parts tend to creep in on a regular basis. There are some parts that are so important to the code that we need to spend some time on them now. Some of the basics that are found in many of your Python codes, and are necessary if you would like to be able to write the proper code in Python, includes

The keywords

The first thing that we need to take a look at is the keywords that are used in this kind of language. These keywords need to be reserved and seen as special because they are in charge of telling the compiler what it needs to do. You do not want to try and use any of these keywords in the wrong manner, or in the wrong place, in the code because then the compiler will have no idea what it is supposed to do.

These keywords have one job, and that is to give the command to the compiler, ensuring that the compiler knows what it is supposed to do when you execute that command. They are so important to all of the codes that you do, so double check the codes that you are writing and ensure that these keywords end up where they are supposed to inside.

Naming the identifiers

The next part of the code that we need to take some time to look at in Python is going to be the identifiers. There are actually quite a few of these that you may work with, even though they come under different names like classes, entities, variables, and functions. Any time that you want to go through and name one of these identifiers, be happy to know that the rules are going to apply to all of them, which means that once you learn the rules for naming the functions, you will be set with the same rules for all of the others.

So, what are some of the rules that you need to follow? First, we need to be careful about the name that we are giving them. There are a lot of names that you can choose, and you get to keep your options open. You can choose from all letters, both big and small, as well as any number that you would like, an underscore symbol, and any combination of the above that you would like to work with.

One thing to remember is the order of these when you are naming. First, you can't start any of the names with a number, and there can't be any spaces that show up between the words that you are writing out. This means that you can't write out something like 4kids or four kids, but you could write out "fourkids" or four_kids," to name that identifier. Also, be careful that you are not using any of the keywords in the names that you are giving to these.

When you come up with the name that you want to give to that identifier, make sure that you remember what it is. It may follow all of the rules that you need, but if you are not able to remember the name when it is time to execute the code or pull out that identifier later on, then there can be some issues. If you call it the wrong thing or you spell it differently, then there could be an error or the compiler is going to get confused.

With that in mind, if you pick a name that makes sense for the identifier that you are working with, and you make sure to follow the rules that you talked about above, then you are going to be just fine, and the code will work the way that you would like.

What is the control flow?

The control flow in this language can be important. This control flow is there to ensure that you wrote out the code the proper way. There are some types of strings in your code that you may want to write out so that the compiler can read them the right way. But if you write out the string in the wrong manner, you are going to end up with errors in the system. We will take a look at many codes int his guidebook that follows the right control flow for this language, which can make it easier to know what you need to get done and how you can write out codes in this language.

Working with the statements

Statements are pretty simple in Python. These are just the strings of code that you write out and that you want the compiler to list out on the string. When you tell the compiler the instructions that you want it to work on, you will find that those are the statements of your code. As long as you write them out properly, the compiler will read them and show up the message that you want on your screen. The statements can be as short or as long as you would like, depending on the code that you are working on.

Comments

The next thing that we are going to take a look at is the comments. There are going to be times when you are writing out a code in Python ad you will want to include an explanation or a note about what you are writing in this code. These notes aren't going to influence how the program works, and you don't want them to even be noticed by your program, but it can help you, and other programmers read the code and know better what is going on in the process.

It is pretty easy to add in these comments the way that you would like this language. You simply need to add the symbol of # ahead of the comment that you are writing. This is going to tell the compiler that you are working on one of these comments and the program, or the compiler is just going to avoid the comment and move on to the next part of the code.

As the coder, you are able to add in as many of these comments to the code as you would like to help explain out the code you are writing, and to keep things flowing nicely. It is actually possible to add one in every other line if you would like, though you want to keep these down a bit to just the ones that are most necessary for your code to work in the proper manner. But as long as you add in that # symbol to the front of the statement, you are able to add in any of these comments, and the compiler will know that you want it to just skip over that part.

The variables

Variables are an important part of the code that you should focus on with the Python code because they are actually really common in the codes that you will write. The variables are there to help you store some of the different values that you place inside of the Python code, and it ensures that the different lines of the code are going to be organized and easy to read through.

Adding the value that you would like to have with the variables is going to be easy to do. You just need to place the equal sign between the variable and the value and the compiler will know what to do. It is even possible for you to use this idea with a few values going to the same variable if you would like. If you take a moment to look through a lot of the codes that we have in this guidebook, and you will see a ton of variables that are going to show up.

Operators

And the last part of the Python code that we need to explore here is going to be the operators. They are pretty simple to work with, but can really make a difference in the way your code works. You will find that there are many options when it comes to the types of operators that you can work with. You may use the arithmetic operators to add together a few parts of the code. You can even work with the operators for assigning values over to the variable that you want to work with. And there are comparison operators that can help the programmer to compare more than one part of the code together and see how they work together and what should happen next in the code.

As you can see with this chapter, there are many parts that can come into play when you are writing your own Python codes. These basics may be simple, but they are going to be found in many of the different codes that we are going to write in this guidebook, even the ones that are a bit more complicated to work on. Learning how to use them, and recognizing them as we work through a lot of the different options and codes that we focus on will make a world of difference in how comfortable you are when it comes time to execute your own codes.

Chapter 4: Classes and Objects

Classes and objects are one of the next things to learn how to do when you work with the Python code. Classes and objects are important to learn how to do because they are going to help you to sort through some of the different parts that come in your code, and will ensure that they are found in the right spots, without any movement when it is time to execute the code that you are working on.

The objects are going to be there in order to define the parts of the code, making it easier for you to understand what you are writing and creating. But then you need to also have the classes there to help store the objects without them moving around. With that in mind, it is time to take a closer look at the closes, and some of the things that you can do to make sure they are created in the proper manner inside of your code.

How can I create a class?

When we are working with Python, you will need to know how to create these classes on your own. This is so important because it will ensure that your code is organized well and that none of the objects are going to end up lost. To make one of these classes though, you need to be able to use the right keywords before you name the class.

Now you are going to get some freedom with this one. You are able to give the class any kind of name that you would like. But remember that it must come after the keyword, and you need to give it a name that you are able to remember later on.

After you give a particular class the name that it needs, you then need to name the subclass that comes with it. You will have this subclass located inside the parenthesis of the code as well. Make sure that when you are done with the first line of the code where you are creating a class, add in a semicolon. This isn't a necessity all of the time, and it is going to still work and execute for you the way you want without it. But it is considered part of the coding etiquette to include this.

Working on one of these classes may seem a bit more complicated, but if you just consider it like a box that is able to hold onto some of the objects that you have, then it makes more sense and is a bit easier to work with. Let's take a look at the syntax that you are able to work with when creating a class, and when that is done, we will look at some of these parts, so we know why things are in certain places.

The code that you need for this includes:

```
class Vehicle(object):
#constructor
def_init_(self, steering, wheels, clutch, breaks, gears):
self._steering = steering
self._wheels = wheels
self._clutch = clutch
self._breaks =breaks
self._gears  = gears
#destructor
def_del_(self):
    print("This is destructor....")


#member functions or methods
def Display_Vehicle(self):
  print('Steering:' , self._steering)
  print('Wheels:', self._wheels)
  print('Clutch:', self._clutch)
  print('Breaks:', self._breaks)
  print('Gears:', self._gears)
#instantiate a vehicle option
myGenericVehicle = Vehicle('Power Steering', 4, 'Super
Clutch', 'Disk Breaks', 5)

myGenericVehicle.Display_Vehicle()
```

Before we move on with this one, we need to take the time to add this into a compiler and see what happens. Just open up the text editor that you are working with and type up the code that we have above. As you write this out, see if you are able to recognize a few of the different topics that we have discussed already in this guidebook! Once you have finished typing this code in, it is time to look at the different parts.

First, it is important to look for the class definition that shows up in this. This class definition is going to be where you are able to instantiate the object, and then you will add in the definition back to the class. This is important because it ensures that you are going to have the right syntax that goes with your code.

For the class definition, you need to pay attention to it because it is responsible for telling the compiler what it should do. If you would like to get a new definition of the class added to the code, you can use the functions of object_method and object_attribute to help you get this done.

The second thing that we should look with when we want to program these classes is going to be the special attributes. These special attributes are important because they are going to provide you with some peace of mind that they will go where you would like without messing things up. The code that we did before is going to have a few examples of these special attributes, but a few more that you may want to spend some time learning and memorizing will include:

__bases__: this is considered a tuple that contains any of the superclasses
__module__: this is where you are going to find the name of the module, and it will also hold your classes.
__name__: this will hold on to the class name.
__doc__: this is where you are going to find the reference string inside the document for your class.
__dict__: this is going to be the variable for the dict. Inside the class name.

Now that we know a bit more about the special attributes, we also need to look at how you are able to access a few of the members that come in that newly created class. You want to ensure that the text editor, as well as the compiler, are able to recognize this new class that you just did. If it can't do that, then there are going to be some errors that come with it.

To make this work, then the code has to go through and be set up in the proper manner. There are a few methods that you are able to do to ensure that this will work. The assessor method is going to be the perfect way to get all of this to come together.

To see how you can access the members of any class that you created, let's take a look at the code you can use below:

```
class Cat(object)
        itsAge = None
        itsWeight = None
        itsName = None
        #set accessor function use to assign values to the fields
or member vars
        def setItsAge(self, itsAge):
        self.itsAge = itsAge

        def setItsWeight(self, itsWeight):
        self.itsWeight = itsWeight

        def setItsName(self, itsName):
        self.itsName =itsName

        #get accessor function use to return the values from a
field
        def getItsAge(self):
        return self.itsAge
        def getItsWeight(self):
        return self.itsWeight

        def getItsName(self):
```

```
    return self.itsName


objFrisky = Cat()
objFrisky.setItsAge(5)
objFrisky.setItsWeight(10)
objFrisky.setItsName("Frisky")
print("Cats Name is:", objFrisky.getItsname())
print("Its age is:", objFrisky.getItsAge())
print("Its weight is:", objFrisky.getItsName())
```

Before we move on, type this into your compiler. If you have your compiler run this, you are going to get some results that show up on the screen right away. This will include that the cat's name is Frisky (or you can change the name to something else if you want), that the age is 5 and that the weight is 10. This is the information that was put into the code, so the compiler is going to pull them up to give you the results that you want. You can take some time to add different options into the code and see how it changes over time.

Classes are not meant to be difficult to work with. They are perfect for helping you to take care of your information and keep it in order so that it makes the most sense. You can create any kind of class that you would like and fill it up with any objects that you like, as long as those objects match each other in some way. Both the objects and classes are going to make a difference in your code to keep it organized, easy to read, and working properly.

Chapter 5: Working with the Exceptions

The next thing that we need to take a look at when it comes to the Python language is how you can work with your own exceptions. We are going to look at how you can handle the ones that the program is going to raise on its own, and the ones that you choose to work on yourself. Understanding how each of these works will help you to write the kinds of codes that you want.

As you are doing your codes, you are going to find that there are going to be certain exceptions that the code is able to bring out on its own. And then there are going to be some exceptions that will fit in with your code well and that you will want to raise on your own. An example of an exception that your code may try to write on its own would be any time the user will divide by zero. The libraries with Python are not going to let this happen. But if you would like to limit what the user is able to do just in that code, then you would need to raise some of your own exceptions.

With the former that we talked about, you will find that the compiler is going to be able to recognize the exceptions all on its own. If the user does one of these things, then the computer or the program is going to recognize that this is going on, and it won't let the program continue. This could be something like dividing by zero or adding in an improper statement, and even when you misspell something on either end of the code and the compiler is not able to find it. Any time that these happen, the program is going to figure out how to handle it all on its own.

As a programmer, it is important to already have a few of the examples of exceptions because they are going to be used quite a bit and they are going to be found in the library for Python. Knowing these ahead of time will help you to know what to add into the code, and will alert you ahead of time when you will see one of these exceptions or not. Some of the exceptions and the keywords that are going to come with them, in the Python code will include:

- Finally—this is the action that you will want to use to perform cleanup actions, whether the exceptions occur or not.
- Assert—this condition is going to trigger the exception inside of the code
- Raise—the raise command is going to trigger an exception manually inside of the code.
- Try/except—this is when you want to try out a block of code and then it is recovered thanks to the exceptions that either you or the Python code raised.

How to raise your own exceptions

The first thing that we need to work on here is how to work with any exceptions that would show up in the code. When one of these exceptions automatically shows up in the code, it is important for you to be prepared and know the steps that you can take to make them more understandable and more. If you are working on a code, and you notice that there is a type of issue that shows up, or you are stuck trying to figure out the reason that the program is doing something that doesn't seem quite right to you, then you will be able to look at the exception that is raised and figure out why.

When these exceptions are raised, it is due to the fact that the program looked through the code that you wrote, and is confused about what you would like it to accomplish for you. Many times, the issue is going to be something that is easy for you to solve and handle. Maybe you are trying to get the program to bring up a file, and you gave it the wrong name. The program was not able to find it, and then it failed because the name was wrong.

A good way to start to see how these exceptions work is to take some time to do our own example and then see what happens when the compiler raises one of these exceptions. Here is a code that you can add into your compiler to see what happens.

```
x = 10
y = 10
result = x/y #trying to divide by zero
print(result)
```

The output that you are going to get when you try to get the interpreter to go through this code would be:

```
>>>
Traceback (most recent call last):
        File "D: \Python34\tt.py", line 3, in <module>
        result = x/y
ZeroDivisionError: division by zero
>>>
```

After you get a chance to look at this example, the compiler will then bring up an error. This is simply due to the fact that the user is trying to divide itself by zero. This is not something that the Python code, or any other coding language for that matter, is going to allow, so the error is going to be raised in the process.

Now, as you see in the code, the error message that is going to be left behind is going to look kind of messy. And it is likely that your users, who are not programmers on their own anyway, are not going to really understand what all is said in that exception message. This message is hard to understand, and it is likely that they are going to have no idea what they are able to do next.

The neat thing that you are able to do here is work to change up the message and ensure that you are going to be able to have your user understand what is going on. You want to make sure that the user understands what is going on when it comes with the exception being raised, rather than having them stare at the program not understanding what is going on. A different way that you can work on writing out this code to make sure that everyone is on the same page and understands what is going on with the exception will include the following:

```
x = 10
y = 0
result = 0
try:
        result = x/y
        print(result)
except ZeroDivisionError:
        print("You are trying to divide by zero.")
```

As you can see, the code that we just put into the compiler is going to be pretty similar to the one that we wrote above. But we did go through and change up the message to show something there when the user raises this exception. When they do get this exception, they will see the message "You are trying to divide by zero" come up on the screen. This isn't a necessary step, but it definitely makes your code easier to use!

How to make some of your own exceptions in the code

Now, with some of the work that we did above, we were just handling some of the exceptions that the code is already going to recognize, ones that will stop the program and are found in the Python library. We had a chance to see how these would work (if you added them into the compiler and tried them out), and even how to change up the message that is going to be shown to your user.

After that is done, it is time to work with some of our own exceptions and see how this can be done, based on the kind of code that you would like to write. There are going to be times when you are working on your own code and programs, and you will want to have the chance to raise a few exceptions all on your own. These may not have anything wrong with them, but to get your program to work the way that you would like, it is important that they show up and do the work.

For example, maybe you want to do a math program, where only certain numbers are going to be the right answers. You don't want the user to put in all sorts of answers and think they are current when only one is the right one. Or you could limit the number of chances that the user gets in order to guess the right answer. Either way, you would need to go through and raise an exception to make sure this works the way that you want.

These are unique exceptions, ones that you should work with to make your code work the way that you want. However, if you don't take the time to actually write them into your code, then the compiler is just going to keep going, without knowing that it should stop or raise the exception. A good example of this, of writing your own exception, would be:

```
class CustomException(Exception):
def_init_(self, value):
        self.parameter = value
def_str_(self):
        return repr(self.parameter)

try:
```

raise CustomException("This is a CustomError!")
except CustomException as ex:
    print("Caught:", ex.parameter)

When you finish this particular code, you are done successfully adding in your own exception. When someone does raise this exception, the message "Caught: This is a CustomError!" will come up on the screen. You can always change the message to show whatever you would like, but this was there as a placeholder to show what we are doing. Take a moment here to add this to the compiler and see what happens.

Exception handling is something that you will work with a lot more as you start to write out some more advanced codes on Python. There are a lot of times that you will work either with the exceptions that are recognized by the program or ones that you want to bring up for the code that you are writing in particular. Working with some of the codes that we bring up in this chapter will help you to deal with these exceptions and will ensure that you are able to make them look good to the user. Make sure to try a few of these codes in your compiler to ensure that you get some practice with these exceptions and that you are able to get a good idea of how these exceptions are supposed to work.

Chapter 6: The If Statements

Next on the list is going to be the if statements. These are sometimes called the decision control statements and conditional statements. There are some times when you will want your program or code to do some things, and even make some decisions, when you are not there to control what it is doing. Any time that the user is allowed to put in some answers on their own, rather than having them pick from one or two options, then these decision control statements are going to be used to help you ensure the program knows how to react with the different answers and keep it moving on.

There are actually a few options when it is time to work with these conditional statements. And the one that you decide to use is going to depend on the kind of code that you are writing as well. The three main options that a programmer is able to use here include the if statement, the if else statement, and the elif statement.

The first option that we are going to take some time to look at is the if statement. These are the easiest and the simplest form of these kinds of statements. And while it is likely that you are not going to use them too often, it is still a good thing for you to learn how these if statements work and to give you some of the basics before we move on to some of the things that are a bit more complicated.

This kind of conditional statement is going to be based on the idea that the user is going to give an answer that is either true or false. If the user puts in the information that the program sees as true, then it is going to continue on with the program and shows the message or other information that you would like. But if the answer that the user gives the computer is seen as false, then the program is going to pause and not go on. As you can see, there are a few issues with this kind of statement, but it is still important to use this to help you get started.

A good way to see how this is going to be able to work for your needs, and how to make sure that you are getting the gist of this kind of conditional statement, we need to look at the following statement:

age = int(input("Enter your age:"))
if (age <=18):
       print("You are not eligible for voting, try next
election!")
print("Program ends")

Let's explore what is going to happen with this code when you put it into your program. If the user comes to the program and puts that they are younger than 18, then there will be a message that shows up on the screen. In this case, the message is going to say "You are not eligible for voting, try next election!" Then the program, as it is, is going to end. But what will happen to this code if the user puts in some age that is 18 or above?

With the if statement, nothing will happen if the user says that their age is above 18. The if statement just has one option and will focus on whether the answer that the user provides is going to match up with the conditions that you set with your code. The user has to put in that they are under the age of 18 with the if statement in this situation, or you won't be able to get the program to happen again.

Now, as you can imagine with the example that we did above, there are some times when this is going to be problematic. You want to make sure that the user puts in the answer that fits the best with their age, and you don't want the program to freeze up or stop just because you only have an answer in place for a certain age group. This is why the traditional if the statement is going to be seen as too simple, and it is time to move on to something else that can handle a little bit more.

The next type of conditional statement that we are going to take a look at, and can help you out more is the if else statement. With these statements, we are going to take a look at the idea that we talked about with the code above, and then we will make sure that there is going to be a response from the program, no matter what age the user is when they get on the program.

You are able to separate people out based on their age, maybe with two groups of those over 19 and those under, or even split them up based on a few different age groups. We are first going to take a look at the code below to see how you would be able to split up the age groups in two:

```
age = int(input("Enter your age:"))
if (age <=18):
        print("You are not eligible for voting, try next election!")
else
        print("Congratulations! You are eligible to vote. Check out your local polling station to find out more information!)
print("Program ends")
```

As you can see, this really helps to add some more options to your code and will ensure that you get an answer no matter what results the user gives to you. You can also change up the message to say anything that you want, but the same idea will be used no matter the answer that the user gives.

You have the option to add in some more possibilities to this. You are not limited to just two options as we have above. If this works for your program, that is just fine to use. But if you need to use more than these two options, you can expand out this as well. For example, take the option above and expand it to have several different age groups. Maybe you want to have different options come for those who are under 18, those that are between the ages of 18 and 30, and those who are over the age of 30. You can separate it out in that way, and when the program gets the answer from the user, it will execute the part that you want.

We can take this idea a little bit further as well. Let's say that you are setting up a program where a user is able to pick out the color that is their favorite. There really isn't a true or false answer to this one, and there are a lot of different options that you are able to pick from when it is time to pick your favorite color, and you do not want to limit people on this one, but you can't list out all of the colors.

For this program, you would use the code that we had above. And maybe pick out six different colors like orange, purple, blue, yellow, green, blue and yellow. You can also have an else at the end that is going to catch all of the other colors that the user may decide to put into the code. Then, the user is able to pick any of the colors of the rainbow that they want. If they pick a color that you did not include in your if part of the statement, then the final statement, or the part with the "else' of this code, will show up.

If you are working with this kind of conditional statement, then you need to make sure that the "else' part of the code is set up in the proper manner. This will ensure that you are still going to be able to get an answer for the user, even if they are not picking out something that you already provided as an option for these conditional statements.

This is a good exampled of an extended out if else statement because there is no way that you a list out all of the colors that are out there. And it would take too long for you to be able to do this anyway. Adding in that conditional statement is going to make it a lot easier for you to cover all of the colors that a user could potentially ask for.

The if-else statement is going to be so important to work within many of your codes. It allows the computer or the program to know how you would like it to react to a lot of different situations based on the answer that the user gives out. And the program or computer is able to do this, even if you are not there, or if you are not able to guess (or don't want to guess) all of the different options that the user may decide to go with.

Now it is time for the elif statements

We spent some time talking about the two other conditional statements that you may choose to go with when you work in Python. The if statements are simple and will just work on the basic true or false options that you may want to work with here. They are simple, but they are a great way to practice conditional statements. The if-else statement is going to take this a bit further and explore the different answers that the user is going to explore during the program.

And now it is time to move on to what is known as the elif statement. The elif statements are going to be a new thing that you are able to work with when it comes to working on the Python code. A good way to think about this is that the user is able to go to this part of your program, and you will present them with a few choices that they can pick from. You can then have certain things happen based on which option the user decides to go with. You can add on as many or as few of these choices for the user to pick from as you would like.

There are a lot of different places where one of these elif statements are going to show up in your code. One of these options could be the menu option on a game. Any time that you get to make some choices of what you would like to do next on the game, or maybe even the things that you would like to purchase through the game, you will most likely be working with an elif statement.

You will find that these elif statements are going to provide you with a number of freedoms. You are allowed to have as many of these statements in your code as you would like. You just have to make sure that you write out the code in the right manner, and you have to make sure the functions are there as well. In addition, if you decide to put in too many of these kinds of statements, then it is going to make it harder to write and can confuse the user.

There are a lot of times when you will find the elif statement is going to work well for you. But you have to ensure that you are using it in the proper manner. A good example of the syntax that goes with these elif statements is right below

if expression1:
statement(s)
elif expression2:
statement(s)
elif expression3:
statement(s)
else:
statement(s)

This is a pretty basic syntax of the elif statement and you can add in as many of these statements as you would like. Just take that syntax and then place the right information into each part and the answer that is listed next to it. Notice that there is also an else statement at the end of this. Don't forget to add this to your code so that it can catch any answer that the user puts in that isn't listed in your elif statements.

To help you better understand how these elif statements work and how the syntax above is going to work, let's take a look at a little game that you can create using these statements:

Print("Let's enjoy a Pizza! Ok, let's go inside Pizzahut!")
print("Waiter, Please select Pizza of your choice from the menu")
pizzachoice = int(input("Please enter your choice of Pizza:"))
if pizzachoice == 1:
print('I want to enjoy a pizza napoletana')
elif pizzachoice == 2:
print('I want to enjoy a pizza rustica')
elif pizzachoice == 3:
print('I want to enjoy a pizza capricciosa')
else:
print("Sorry, I do not want any of the listed pizza's, please bring a Coca Cola for me.")

When you use this kind of code, you will be able to allow the user to make any choices that they want, and then, as long as this is set up in the proper manner, they are going to get the right option to meet up with them as well. For example, if they want to go with the pizza rustica, they will pick the number 2. If they want to have just a drink rather than one of the other choices above, they can do that too. While we did use the example of pizza in here, there are a lot of other things that you can do with it, so pretty much if you want your user to have some options, you would use the syntax that is above and then fills in the options that work the best for you.

The conditional statements are great options to work with because they provide you with a lot more power than you can get with some of the other options in coding. It is a great way to make sure that you are able to make a program that can make decisions, without you having to come up with every possible scenario and without you having to be there to make the decisions as well. Try out a few of these conditional statements in your compiler and experiment a bit to see all the amazing things that you can do with this conditional statement.

Chapter 7: Creating Inheritances in the Python Language

Working with some inheritances in your code can make a big difference in how things line up and work. In fact, these inheritances are going to be a good way to enhance any of the codes that you would like to work within Python. They are going to come into the code and save you a lot of time, while still ensuring that your code looks clean and nice along the way. Any programmer is able to do this by reusing a part of their previous code, without having to go through and rewrite the same code over and over again.

Basically, when you are ready to work with an inheritance in Python, it is time to take the original code, which is going to be known as the parent code here, and then change up parts of it before you reuse it in the derived or the child class. You are able to make any of the changes that you need to the child class to get it to work the way that you would like. Even as someone who is just starting with the Python process, you will be able to use the inheritances to help you rewrite different parts of your code over and over again.

During one of these inheritances, you are going to take the parent code, which is that original code, and copy it over into a new part of the program. This is then going to be the child code. With this child code, you can mess around with it and make it stronger or make other changes as you would wish. In some cases, you will want to copy it down as it is, and other times you may want to change up something inside of it to make the code work the way that you would like it to work.

To make a bit more sense out of some of the inheritances that you can do, and even out of how you can work with these inheritances, let's take a moment here to look at the code below to see exactly how these will work:

```
#Example of inheritance
#base class
class Student(object):
        def __init__(self, name, rollno):
        self.name = name
        self.rollno = rollno
#Graduate class inherits or derived from Student class
class GraduateStudent(Student):
        def __init__(self, name, rollno, graduate):
        Student__init__(self, name, rollno)
        self.graduate = graduate

def DisplayGraduateStudent(self):
        print"Student Name:", self.name)
```

```
        print("Student Rollno:", self.rollno)
        print("Study Group:", self.graduate)


#Post Graduate class inherits from Student class
class PostGraduate(Student):
        def __init__(self, name, rollno, postgrad):
        Student __init__(self, name, rollno)
        self.postgrad = postgrad

        def DisplayPostGraduateStudent(self):
        print("Student Name:", self.name)
        print("Student Rollno:", self.rollno)
        print("Study Group:", self.postgrad)


#instantiate from Graduate and PostGraduate classes
        objGradStudent = GraduateStudent("Mainu", 1, "MS-
Mathematics")
        objPostGradStudent = PostGraduate("Shainu", 2, "MS-
CS")
        objPostGradStudent.DisplayPostGraduateStudent()
```

When you type this into your interpreter, you are going to get the results:

```
('Student Name:', 'Mainu')
('Student Rollno:', 1)
```

('Student Group:', 'MSC-Mathematics')

('Student Name:', 'Shainu')

('Student Rollno:', 2)

('Student Group:', 'MSC-CS')

Overriding one of your base classes

Now that we have an example in code form above about what the inheritance is going to look like, now we need to take a look at what you would do when you want to take the base class and override it. There are going to be times when you have a new class, a child class, and you want to be able to override it a bit and change up some of the features in it to get it to work the way that you would like.

To make this happen, without making a mess along the way, you have to take a look at some of the things that are inside of the base class, and then determine how you can change those a bit to get that new child class. The child class is then going to work in order to use that new behavior to get the job done for you.

This may sound a bit scary to someone who is just getting started with the idea of inheritances and more, but it is really nice because you get a lot of freedom to pick out which parental features to keep around and which ones need to be avoided. This process, with the coding that we have above and more, is going to really help you to make all of the changes that you want with the child class, while still maintaining the parts that you do not want to change.

The number of times that you decide to do this is going to depend on the kind of code that you decide to work with. And you can make changes each time that you would like to make this happen. You can go through and have ten of these going down the line if you would like. And you can make it as simple or as complicated as you would like for your program. Putting it all together, and learning the basic steps to get all of this started is the trick that you need to ensure that you see the best results, and can add in as many of these layers as you would like.

Chapter 8: Can I Create a Loop

Creating loops can be another great thing that you can work on when you have the Python language. These loops are going to make your life a whole lot easier, and often they can work well with the conditional statements that we talked about above in terms of making sure your code works the way that you want. Loops will speed up how long it takes to write your codes, can clean it all up, and can take hundreds of lines of code and wraps it up into just a few lines if you do it in the proper manner. Even as a beginner, you are able to make these loops work for you, so let's take a look at the way that you are able to make these works for your needs.

You will find that these loops are going to be so helpful any time that you are writing out a code where you would like to get a certain part of the program to go over and over the same lines, at least two times but often many, but you don't want to waste your time and make your code really messy by writing out the code each time. Let's say that you are going to try and write out a code for a multiplication chart to 100. Maybe you would write it all out line by line and waste a lot of time while making your code a mess. Or you could use a loop and write it out in just a few lines (we will show you how to do this in a little bit).

While this is something that can seem pretty complex, you will find that even as a beginner, it is really easy to work with these looks. The way that these kinds of code are going to work along with the compiler is that they are going to tell the compiler to just repeat the same part of the code over and over again. It is going to do this as many times as is needed, or until the condition that you added into the code ends up being met.

If you would like your code to have the ability to count up from one to ten, then you would simply need to tell the compiler that you want it to be able to stop once it gets to the number ten. We will look at a few of the examples that you can use to make all of this happen as we go through this guidebook.

Of course, when you are ready to start writing out these loops, you need to make sure that the conditions are set up the right way. if you don't set up your condition right from the beginning, then the program is going to end up with a mess because the code won't know when to stop, and it will keep going through the code an endless number of times, making you get stuck in a continuous loop. You have to put the condition put into the code, so it knows when you need it to stop and move on to the next part of the code.

When you work with what may be considered traditional methods of coding, or the ones that we talked about earlier on in this guidebook, your goal would be to write out all of the lines of code that you need. Even if there are some parts of the code that seem to be really similar, you would still need to go through and retype the same part of the code over and over again until it was done. But with loops, this is something that is no longer a concern.

Any time that you bring out the loops, you can dump the traditional way of doing coding out the window. You are able to combine many of the lines of code and make them work with just a few lines if you would like. The compiler will still be able to handle this and will know to repeat the lines as many times as you would like, as long as those conditions are all put in place.

With that introduction to the loops, it is time to look at the different types that you may work with when you start using the Python coding language. Some of the options include the for loop, the while loop, and the nested loop and we are going to take some time to go through each of these and see how each of them works and how they are going to improve your code writing.

What is the while loop?

The first type of loop that you can work within your Python code is known as the while loop. The while loop is the type that you will use if you want to make sure that the code goes through a cycle a predetermined number of times. You can set this number of times when you write the code to make sure the loop goes for as long as you would like.

With the while loop, your goal is not to make the code go through its cycle an indefinite amount of times, but you do want to make sure that it goes through for a specific number of times. If you are counting from one to ten, you want to make sure it goes through the loop ten times to be right. With this option, the loop is going to go through at least one time and then check to see if the conditions are met or not. So, it will put up the number one, then check its conditions and put up the number two, and so on until it sees where it is.

To give us a little bit better of an understanding on how these loops work, let's take a look at some sample codes of the while loop and see what happens:

counter = 1
while(counter <= 3):
        principal = int(input("Enter the principal amount:"))

```
numberofyeras = int(input("Enter the number of years:"))
rateofinterest = float(input("Enter the rate of interest:"))
simpleinterest = principal * numberofyears * rateofinterest/100
print("Simple interest = %.2f" %simpleinterest)
#increase the counter by 1
counter = counter + 1
print("You have calculated simple interest for 3 time!")
```

Before we move on, take this code and add it to your compiler and let it execute this code. You will see that when this is done, the output is going to come out in a way that the user can place any information that they want into the program. Then the program will do its computations and figure out the interest rates, as well as the final amounts, based on whatever numbers the user placed into the system.

With this particular example, we set the loop up to go through three times. This allows the user to put in results three times to the system before it moves on. You can always change this around though and add in more of the loops if it works the best for your program.

On to the for loop

Now that we have had a moment to take a look at the while loop, it is time to bring in the for loop and see how this one is going to be able to benefit us in a slightly different manner. The while loop that we just went through is going to have a lot of uses in your Python code. However, there may be times when it is not going to be able to handle all of the things that you want to do, and you may need to work with things in a different manner. And that is when we are going to start looking at them for a loop.

When we are ready for the for loop, you will be setting things up in your code so that the user isn't the one who will get in and give the information that is needed to tell the program to stop running the loop. Instead of having the user in charge, the for loop is going to set up in a way that it will go over the iteration in the order that you place the items in your statement, and then this information will show up in that exact manner. There isn't really a need for the user to input anything, at least until it gets to the end of the code.

A good example of how this is going to work inside your code so that you are able to make it work for your needs will include the following syntax:

```
# Measure some strings:
words = ['apple', 'mango', 'banana', 'orange']
for w in words:
print(w, len(w))
```

When you work with the for loop example that is above, you are able to add it to your compiler and see what happens when it gets executed. When you do this, the four fruits that come out on your screen will show up in the exact order that you have them written out. If you would like to have them show up in a different order, you can do that, but then you need to go back to your code and rewrite them in the right order, or your chosen order. Once you have then written out in the syntax and they are ready to be executed in the code, you can't make any changes to them.

And finally, the nested loop

And then there is one final loop type that we are going to need to work within our Python code is the nested loop. You will find that the nested loop can use some of the parts that we have talked about with the for loop and the while loop but in a slightly different manner. When you are bringing out the nested loop, you will basically take one loop and then have it placed right inside of another loop. Then both of the loops will continue on their path until they are both able to finish.

This may seem like it is really complicated to get started with, and you may be wondering at this time when you would actually need to use this kind of loop, but you may find that as you get to writing some of your own codes, there are actually quite a few times when this does come in handy. For example, you may have a time when you need to write out a multiplication table inside the code, giving you answers from one times one, all the way up to ten times ten.

Imagine how long this would take to go through and write out each line of code. You would need to write out one time one, one times two, one times three, one times four and so on until you got yourself all the way up to ten times ten. This is a lot of lines of code and can take you forever. But with a nested loop, you are able to get this to work for you, without having to write out so much code at once. A good syntax of how you can write out the multiplication table idea that we talked about before will include

#write a multiplication table from 1 to 10
For x in xrange(1, 11):
     For y in xrange(1, 11):

*Print '%d = %d' % (x, y, x*x)*

When you got the output of this program, it is going to look similar to this:

1*1 = 1
1*2 = 2
1*3 = 3
1*4 = 4
All the way up to 1*10 = 2
Then it would move on to do the table by twos such as this:
2*1 =2
2*2 = 4
And so, on until you end up with 10*10 = 100 as your final spot in the sequence.

Go ahead and put this into the compiler and see what happens. You will simply have four lines of code, and end up with a whole multiplication table that shows up on your program. Think of how many lines of code you would have to write out to get this table the traditional way that you did before? This table only took a few lines to accomplish, which shows how powerful and great the nested loop can be.

The loops are great options to add into your code. There are a lot of reasons when you would need to take a loop and add it inside your code. You will be able to use it as a way to get a lot of coding done in just a few lines, and a way to clean up the code so that you can still get the same thing done without writing out too much. The compiler is set up to keep reading through the loop until the condition that you set is no longer valid. This can open up a lot of things that you are able to do with your code, while also keeping things clean and manageable all at the same time.

Chapter 9: Working with the Python Files

The next thing that we need to focus on when it comes to working with Python is making sure we know how to do with these kinds of codes is working with the Python files. There are going to be times when you are working with some data in these codes, and you will want to store it then while ensuring that it is accessible for you to pull up and use when the data is needed later. You do have some choices in the way that you save this data, how it is going to be found later on, and how it is going to react in your code.

When you work with the files, you will find that the data is going to be saved on a disk, or you are able to re-use in the code over and over again as much as you would like. This chapter is going to help us learn a bit more about how to handle some of the work that we need to do to ensure the files behave the way that they should, and so much more.

Now, we are going to enter into file mode on the Python language, and this allows you to do a few different options along the way. A good way to think about this is that you can think about it like working on a file in Word. At some point, you may try to save one of the documents that you are working with so that it doesn't get lost and you are able to find them later on. These kinds of files in Python are going to be similar. But you won't be saving pages as you did on Word, you are going to save parts of your code.

You will find with this one that there are a few operations or methods that you are able to choose when it comes to working with files. And some of these options will include:

1. Closing up a file you are working on.
2. Creating a brand new file to work on.
3. Seeking out or moving a file that you have over to a new location to make it easier to find.
4. Writing out a new part of the code on a file that was created earlier.

Creating your new files

The first task that we are going to look at doing here is working on creating a file. It is hard to do much of the other tasks if we don't first have a file in place to help us out. if you would like to be able to make a new file and then add in some code into it, you first need to make sure the file is opened up inside of your IDLE. Then you can choose the mode that you would like to use when you write out your code.

When it comes to creating files on Python, you will find there are three modes that you are able to work with. The three main modes that we are going to focus on here includes append (a), mode(x) and write(w).

Any time that you would like to open up a file and make some changes in it, then you would want to use the write mode. This is the easiest out of the three to work with. The write method is going to make it easier for you to get the right parts of the code set up and working for you in the end.

The write function is going to be easy to use and will ensure that you are able to make any and all additions and changes that you would like to the file. You can add in the new information that you would like to the file, change what is there, and so much more. If you would like to see what you are able to do with this part of the code with the write method, then you will want to open up your compiler and do the following code:

```
#file handling operations
#writing to a new file hello.txt
f = open('hello.txt', 'w', encoding = 'utf-8')
f.write("Hello Python Developers!")
f.write("Welcome to Python World")
f.flush()
```

f.close()

From here, we need to discuss what you are able to do with the directories that we are working with. The default directory is always going to be the current directory. You are able to go through and switch up the directory where the code information is stored, but you have to take the time, in the beginning, to change that information up, or it isn't going to end up in the directory that you would like.

Whatever directory you spent your time in when working on the code is the one you need to make your way back to when you want to find the file later on. If you would like it to show up in a different directory, make sure that you move over to that one before you save it and the code. With the option that we wrote above, when you go to the current directory (or the directory that you chose for this endeavor, then you will be able to open up the file and see the message that you wrote out there.

For this one, we wrote a simple part of the code. You, of course, will be writing out codes that are much more complicated as we go along. And with those codes, there are going to be times when you would like to edit or overwrite some of what is in that file. This is possible to do with Python, and it just needs a small change to the syntax that you are writing out. A good example of what you are able to do with this one incudes:

```
#file handling operations
#writing to a new file hello.txt
f = open('hello.txt', 'w', encoding = 'utf-8')
f.write("Hello Python Developers!")
f.write("Welcome to Python World")
mylist = ["Apple", "Orange", "Banana"]
#writelines() is used to write multiple lines in to the file
f.write(mylist)
f.flush()
f.close()
```

The example above is a good one to use when you want to make a few changes to a file that you worked on before because you just need to add in one new line. This example wouldn't need to use that third line because it just has some simple words, but you can add in anything that you want to the program, just use the syntax above and change it up for what you need.

What are the binary files?

One other thing that we need to focus on for a moment before moving on is the idea of writing out some of your files and your data in the code as a binary file. This may sound a bit confusing, but it is a simple thing that Python will allow you to do. All that you need to do to make this happen is to take the data that you have and change it over to a sound or image file, rather than having it as a text file.

With Python, you are able to change any of the code that you want into a binary file. It doesn't matter what kind of file it was in the past. But you do need to make sure that you work on the data in the right way to ensure that it is easier to expose in the way that you want later on. The syntax that is going to be needed to ensure that this will work well for you will be below:

 # write binary data to a file
 # writing the file hello.dat write binary mode
F = open('hello.dat', 'wb')
 # writing as byte strings
f.write(b"I am writing data in binary file!/n")
f.write(b"Let's write another list/n")
f.close()

If you take the time to use this code in your files, it is going to help you to make the binary file that you would like. Some programmers find that they like using this method because it helps them to really get things in order and will make it easier to pull the information up when you need it.

Opening your file up

So far, we have worked with writing a new file and getting it saved, and working with a binary file as well. In these examples, we got some of the basics of working with files down so that you are able to make them work for you and you can pull them up any time that you would like.

Now that this part is done, it is time to learn how to open up the file and use it, and later even make changes to it, any time that you would like. Once you open that file up, it is going to be so much easier to use it again and again as much as you would like. When you are ready to see the steps that are needed in order to open up a file and use it, you will need the following syntax.

```
# read binary data to a file
#writing the file hello.dat write append binary mode

with open("hello.dat", 'rb') as f:
        data = f.read()
        text = data.decode('utf-8'(
print(text)
```

the output that you would get form putting this into the system would be like the following:

Hello, world!
This is a demo using with
This file contains three lines
Hello world
This is a demo using with

This file contains three lines.

Seeking out a file you need

And finally, we need to take a look at how you are able to seek out some of the files that you need on this kind of coding language. We already looked at how to make the files, how to store them in different manners, how to open them and rewrite on them, and then how to seek the file. But there are times where you are able to move one of the files that you have over to a new location.

For example, if you are working on a file and as you do that, you find that things are not showing up the way that you would like it to, then it is time to fix this up. Maybe you didn't spell the time of the identifier the right way, or the directory is not where you want it to be, then the seek option may be the best way to actually find this lost file and then make the changes, so it is easier to find later on.

With this method, you are going to be able to change up where you place the file, to ensure that it is going to be in the right spot all of the time or even to make it a bit easier for you to find it when you need. You just need to use a syntax like what is above in order to help you make these changes.

Working through all of the different methods that we have talked about in this chapter are going to help you to do a lot of different things inside of your code. Whether you would like to make a new file, you want to change up the code, move the file around, and more; you will be able to do it all using the codes that we have gone through in this chapter.

Chapter 10 The Importance of the Python Functions

Another important topic that you are able to work with in order to see some great results with your codes are going to be the Python functions. These functions are going to be known as a set of expressions, or statements, that will either have a name, or you can choose to keep them a bit anonymous. They are going to be the first types of class objects that you will be able to find inside the code, so you won't have to worry as much about the restrictions or how these functions are going to be allowed to work.

When you decide to pull up these functions or create a new one, you will find that they are pretty similar to other kinds of values that you are using in the code. You will be able to use them like the strings or the numbers that we have talked about before, and you can add-in attributes that help with these, as like as you use the prefix of "dir."

There are a lot of different types of functions that you are able to deal with, and you can even choose from a good variety of attributes when it is time to create, and then later bring up, the functions that you want to use in your code. Some of the different choices that are available to help you with this will include the following:

- __doc__: This is going to return the docstring of the function that you are requesting.
- Func_default: This one is going to return a tuple of the values of your default argument.
- Func_globals: This one will return a reference that points to the dictionary holding the global variables for that function.
- Func_dict: This one is responsible for returning the namespace that will support the attributes for all your arbitrary functions.
- Func_closure: This will return to you a tuple of all the cells that hold the bindings for the free variables inside of the function.

As you can see, working with these functions is not something that has to be extraordinarily hard to work with. It takes some time to add them in, but if you use some of the identifiers that are above, you will be just fine getting this all done.

Chapter 11: Bringing in Some Data Visualization

Another part that we need to take a look at with the Python language is the idea of data visualization. This is a big part of the job of a data scientist. In the early stages of the project, it is likely that you are going to spend a lot of time doing what is known as EDA, or Exploratory Data Analysis, in order to gain a bit more insight into your data.

Being able to create some visualizations can really help make things easier and for you to understand, especially when it comes to data sets that are larger and are seen as higher dimensional. When you are getting close to done with your project, it is also important for you to be able to present these results in a manner that is compelling, concise, and clear so that an audience, even if they are not technically inclined, are able to understand the information as well.

Before we get too far into all of this, you may want to make sure that you have the Python library known as Matplotlib on your system. You will be able to use this to make some of the things that you will do with data visualization a bit easier. However, you may find that setting up the figures, parameters, data, and plotting all of this is going to be tedious and a bit messy if you have to go through and redo them each time you start a new project.

In this chapter, we are going to explore a few different types of data visualizations you can work with, along with some of the easy and fast functions that you can do with each of these thanks to the Matplotlib that you can get form Python. Make sure to get this library on your system, if it is not there already, to help you get this done.

Scatter Plots

The first thing that you can look at with data visualization is the scatter plots. These are going to be great when it is time to show the relationship between two different variables since you can look at them and see the raw distribution of any kind of data that you have. You can also view this relationship for different groups of data if they are split up, simply by changing the color of each ground.

Let's say that you want to take a look at the relationship that is present between three different variables. This is pretty easy to do. You just need to use the parameters to change the colors of each one so that you can split them all up into the groups that you want. Then, thanks to the colors telling us which dots are for each parameter, we are better able to see the relationship that is going to show up here.

So that brings up the question of how you are able to do this with Python. We first need to import the pyplot from Matplotlib. It is going to have the alias of plt. To create a new plot figure, we are going to call up "plt.subplots(). We pass the x-axis and the y-axis data over to the function, and then these are going to be passed over to the ax.scatter() to plot the scatter plot. We can also go through and set up the alpha transparency, the point color, and the point size. You are even able to go through and set up the y-axis so that it comes in with a logarithmic scale. The title and the axis labels are then going to be set in a specific manner that you want.

To see the code that you will want to use to make this happen and to create your own scatter plot (importing the information that you want it to look over), you just need to work with the code that is found below:

import
matplotlib.pyplot as
plt
            import numpy as np

```
def scatterplot(x_data, y_data,
x_label="", y_label="", title="", color =
"r", yscale_log=False):
# Create the plot object
_, ax = plt.subplots()
# Plot the data, set the size (s), color
and transparency (alpha)
# of the points
ax.scatter(x_data, y_data, s = 10, color
= color, alpha = 0.75)
```

Line Plots

The next thing that we are going to take a look at when we are working with Python and data visualization is going to be the line plots. These are going to be the best thing to use when you are able to clearly see that one variable is going to be quite a bit different than the other. This also means they have a high amount of co-variance.

There may be times when you have a lot of different items that you need to work with at the same time. and maybe they touch and meet up at the same points on a regular basis. If you tried to do a scatter plot of all of this information, it would get messy and be hard to look through and analyze at all. The lines, usually in different colors, can still give you an idea of where each type is going, how they can be separated out, and more.

If you would like to be able to make your own line plot with the help of the Python code, then you can use the following code to help you get all of this done:

```
def lineplot(x_data,
y_data, x_label="",
y_label="", title=""):
                                    # Create the plot object
                                    _, ax = plt.subplots()
                                    # Plot the best fit line, set the
                                    linewidth (lw), color and
                                    # transparency (alpha) of the
                                    line
                                    ax.plot(x_data, y_data, lw = 2,
                                    color = '#539caf', alpha = 1)
                                    # Label the axes and provide a
                                    title
                                    ax.set_title(title)
                                    ax.set_xlabel(x_label)
```

Histograms

Another type of data visualization tool that you are able to work with when you are ready to get some great ways to look through your data is going to be the histogram. You will find that these histograms are going to be useful when you are viewing, or when you want to discover, how the data points you are working with are being distributed.

When you are looking at some of these histograms, you may notice that it is going to show you that there is going to be a nice concentration of points that shows up right in the middle, and this is going to be the median that you need to focus on. You will also see that many of these are going to be able to follow what is known as a Gaussian distribution.

When you use the bars that are found in a histogram, rather than the scatter points or even the lines on this one, you are going to really be able to visualize of the relative difference between the frequency of each part. The use of the bins is going to be helpful here because it ensures that you are able to really come in and see the bigger picture. But if there weren't these kinds of bins in place, there would end up being a ton of noise in the visualization, which would make it harder to look through the data and see what is going on there.

We will look at the code that you can use in Matplotlib in order to create one of these histograms. Before we do that, though, there are going to be a few parameters that are important, and we need to take a look at them. The first of these is going to be the n_bins parameter. This is important because it is able to control how many of the discrete bins you want to allow with this histogram.

If you are working with more of these bins, it is going to give you finer information, but it is possible that having too many of these will introduce a lot of noise and can take you away from the bigger picture that you want to have. Then there is the issue with having not enough bins. This is going to give you more of a bird's eye view. It shows you the bigger picture of what might be seen in the data, but without the finer details that you may need.

The second parameter that you need to look at is going to be the cumulative parameter. This is a Boolean one that will allow you to select whether the histogram is considered cumulative or not. This is basically where you are going to pick out the CDF, or the Cumulative Density Function, or the PDF, or the Probability Density Function.

Now we can get to the code. The code that you can use with the Python program to make your own histogram is going to include:

```
def histogram(data, n_bins, cumulative=False, x_label = "",
y_label = "", title = ""):
    _, ax = plt.subplots()
    ax.hist(data, n_bins = n_bins, cumulative = cumulative,
    color = '#539caf')
    ax.set_ylabel(y_label)
    ax.set_xlabel(x_label)
    ax.set_title(title)
```

Now, you may find that there are going to be times when you could bring out the histogram in order to compare how the distribution of the two variables are going to work with the data. You may assume that you have to go through and create two different histograms and look at this information all on its own or compare side to side. But there is actually a way that you are able to do in order to help you out. You can overlay the histograms with varying transparencies to see where they match together and where not.

There are a lot of times when you will want to work with this kind of histogram, but first, you need to make sure that there are a few things set up in the code to do this. First, we need to be able to set up a horizontal range in order to help you deal with both of the distributions. According to the number of bins you want to use and this range, you can then compute the width that you need for each bin. And then you need to work on plotting both of these histograms on the same plot, allowing one of them to show up a bit more transparent than the other so you can compare. The code that you need to make this one happen includes the following:

 # Overlay 2 histograms to compare them

def overlaid_histogram(data1, data2, n_bins = 0,

data1_name="", data1_color="#539caf", data2_name="",

data2_color="#7663b0", x_label="", y_label="", title=""):

 # Set the bounds for the bins so that the two distributions
are fairly compared

max_nbins = 10

data_range = [min(min(data1), min(data2)),
max(max(data1), max(data2))]

binwidth = (data_range[1] - data_range[0]) / max_nbins

if n_bins == 0

bins = np.arange(data_range[0], data_range[1] +
binwidth, binwidth)

else:

Bar Plots

You can also work with bar plots when it comes to working in the Python language. You will find that working on these bar plots can be effective when you are working on visualizing some data that is categorical and has only a few categories, usually less than ten. If you end up with too many categories here, then the bars are going to look cluttered, and it is hard for you to read through this and understand it.

These bar plots are going to be helpful when you want to work with categorical data because you will then be able to look through the categories and find out the comparisons based on the sizes of the bars. You can even take the categories and divide them up based on their color as well. There are going to be three main types of bar plots that you can work with to sort out your data, including stacked, grouped, and regular.

The regular bar plot is the first one that we will be able to look at. In the barplot() function, the x_data is going to represent the tickers on the x-axis, and the y_data is going to be the height of the bar as it goes up the y-axis. The error bar is going to be the extra line centered on each bar that you will be able to draw out and show what the standard deviation is.

Then there is the grouped bar plot. This one is going to be important at times because it helps us to compare more than one variable. The first variable that we are going to go through and compare is going to be the scores that are in each group, using G1, G2, and more. We are also comparing the genders themselves, but we are going to color code them.

When we look at the code in a bit, the y_data_list variable is not actually going to be a list of lists, and you will notice that each sublist that we have is going to be able to show us another group. We can then go through and loop through each group, and then each of these groups is going to have us draw the bar for each tock on the x-axis. These groups are going to be color-coded for us.

And then the third type of bar plot is going to be the stacked bar plot. These are going to be great when it is time to visualize the categorical make-up of the different variables. Om the stacked bar plot we are going to be able to color code it and do more in order to figure out what seemed to work the best on each day or in each category for us.

The codes that are needed to work with the bar plots and to make sure that they work well for your needs will include the following:

```python
def barplot(x_data,
y_data, error_data,
x_label="", y_label="",
title=""):
    _, ax = plt.subplots()
    # Draw bars, position them in the
    center of the tick mark on the x-
    axis
    ax.bar(x_data, y_data, color =
    '#539caf', align = 'center')
    # Draw error bars to show
    standard deviation, set ls to 'none'
    # to remove line between points
    ax.errorbar(x_data, y_data, yerr
    = error_data, color = '#297083', ls
    = 'none', lw = 2, capthick = 2)
    ax.set_ylabel(y_label)
    ax.set_xlabel(x_label)
    ax.set_title(title)
```

Box Plots

We already took some time to look at histograms earlier in this chapter. Histograms are a great way for you to visualize the distribution of variables. But there are going to be some times when you will want to work with some more information than that. Perhaps you would like to be able to find a clearer view of the standard deviation. You may sometimes find the information for the median is going to be quite a bit different from the mean, and it results in a lot of outliers that you need to figure out as well. What if there is such a skew in it and a lot of the values are going to be concentrated to one side.

This is where you will be able to use the boxplots to your advantage. Box plots are going to give it all of the information that you need even if there are a lot of changes that go on in the data. The bottom and the top of these solid lined boxes are going to be the first and the third quartiles, and then the band inside the box is always going to be our median or the second quartile. The whiskers or the dashed lines with bars on the end, are going to extend from the box to show you what range of the data.

Since the box plot that we want to work with is going to be drawn for each group or variable, it is going to be easy to set up. The x_data is going to be a list of the groups and variables.

The Matplotlib function of boxplot() is going to help us make a plot for each of the columns of the y_data or each vector in the sequence y_data. This means that each value that shows up in the x_data is going to correspond to a volume or vector that is in the y_data. All we have to do for this is to set them up to look right in the plot.

Now that we have talked a bit about how the box plot looks like, it is time to take a look at the code that you need to use in order to make all of this happen. The best code to make your own box plot includes

```
def boxplot(x_data, y_data, base_color="#539caf",
median_color="#297083", x_label="", y_label="", title=""):
_, ax = plt.subplots()
# Draw boxplots, specifying desired style
ax.boxplot(y_data
# patch_artist must be True to control box fill
, patch_artist = True
# Properties of median line
, medianprops = {'color': median_color}
# Properties of box
, boxprops = {'color': base_color, 'facecolor': base_color}
```

These are the five things that you can do when it comes to doing data visualization in your work. Abstracting things into functions can always make it easier for you to read your code and use it. And you can use the simple codes that we have in this chapter to help you make some of your own codes and see some amazing results in the process.

Chapter 12: Testing Your Code

When you are working with the Python language, there is some time when you would want to test out the codes that you are working with. Getting used to writing out some of your own testing code, and then running it at the same time that you do with the rest of your code is seen as a good habit in coding, and learning how to do it the right way is going to make sure that you get things to work the way that you want. When you use this kind of method in the proper manner, it is going to make it easier to define your code and get it to work well.

Before we get started, it is important to take a look at a few of the rules that are there for testing to keep things organized. These rules include

1. A testing unit has to focus on just one tiny part of the functionality of your code, and then it needs to prove that this is correct, rather than taking on a really large part.
2. Each test unit needs to be fully independent and on its own. This means that each test that you need to run should be able to run on its own, while also being in the test suite, regardless of the order it is called up. The implication of this kind of rule is that each test has to be

loaded up with a fresh set of data and then it needs to be able to do the cleanup to make this happen. This is usually going to be handled by the methods of setup() and teardown().

3. You should make it a goal to get tests that are able to run fast. If you find that one of your individual's tests ends up needing more than a few milliseconds to run, this is going to slow down your development, or these tests may not run as often as you desire.

   a. In some cases, the tests aren't going to be fast because they need to work on some complex data structure. And then you need to load up this data each time the tests run. If you have to do some of these heavier tasks in your tests, then you need to make sure that they are kept in a separate test suite that is run by some scheduled task, and then run all of the other tests as often as they are needed in all of this.

4. Learn about all of your tools and learn how to run a single test or a test case. Then, when you are developing a function inside of a module, run this function's tests frequently, ideally automatically when you try to save some part of the code.

5. Always make it so that the full test suite is going to run before the coding session, and then have it run again when the coding is done. This is going to ensure that

there is some confidence that nothing will break in the rest of the code and that the cleanup is going to work the way that you want.

6. It is always a good idea to implement a hook that runs all tests before you try to push code to a shared repository.

7. If you are already in the middle of one of your sessions of development and you have to stop, it is still a good idea to go through and write out a broken test about what you would like to have done next. When you come back to the coding later than, this is going to give you a pointer about where you were at that time and can ensure that you are going to be able to get back on track a bit faster.

8. The first thing that should be looked at when you want to debug your code is to write out a new test that pinpoints that bug. While this is not always going to be an easy thing to do, those bug catching tests are going to help you out so much and are one of the most valuable things that you are able to do to keep your code working well.

9. Try to use long and descriptive names for testing functions. The style guide here is going to be a bit different compared to what you are going to do when you run your code, where you will most often want to stay with some shorter names. The reason for this is

that testing the functions are never going to be called up explicitly. Square() and sqr() are ok when you are running the code, but they are not going to be used when you are running a test.

10. When you see that there is something going wrong, or there is something that should be changed, and if your code already has a good set of tests, you or the other maintainers are going to need to work on your testing suite in order to make the modifications or to fix some of the problems. Therefore, this means that you will need to test the code to be read more than the rest. A unit test whose purpose is unclear is not going to help you out with this much.

11. Another way that you are able to use your testing code is a type of introduction to a lot of new developers. When you need to work on the code base, running and reading the related testing code is a great way to help them to start. You will then be able to discover some of the hot pots, where a lot of difficulties can arise. They will be able to add in some functionality and learn a lot more about your code in the process.

Decisions to make before testing

Before you dive into writing your own tests in Python, you want to make up a few decisions as well. You need to figure out what you would like to test and figure out whether you are working with an integration test or a unit test. When you have this figured out, you will then need to structure out the test and how it is loosely going to follow with the workflow. You need it to create the inputs, then you need to move on to the code being tested and capturing your output. And in the end, you need to compare the output with the results that you were expecting to get.

For this kind of application, you may want to test out the sum() method. There are a lot of different things that this kind of method is able to check including:

1. Can it sum a list of whole numbers or integers?
2. Can it sum a tuple or a set?
3. Can it sum a list of floats?
4. What happens when you put in a bad value, such as a single integer or a whole string?
5. What is going to happen when one of the values ends up being negative?

Manual vs. Automated Testing

The good news to consider here is that when writing out some of the codes that you want to work with, it is likely that you have been able to test without realizing it. Remember when you ran the application and used it for the first time? Did you check through the features and experiment using them? This is something that is known as exploratory testing and is a form of manual testing.

Exploratory testing is going to be a form of testing that any coder is able to do without a plan in place. When you are in this kind of testing, you are just going through and exploring the application and all that it is able to do.

To have a complete set of manual tests, all you need to do is make a list of all the features of your application, the different types of input it can accept, and the results that you are expecting. Now, every time you try to make a change to your code, you will need to go through every item that you have added to that list and check it all out.

Of course, this isn't something that sounds like that much fun. You don't really want to go through all of that and try to create some of the code each time. This is where automated testing is going to be able to come in. automated testing is going to be the execution of your test plan (which is the parts of your application that you would like to test, in the order that you wish to test them, and then the responses that you plan to get), but a script rather than the person going through and doing it.

Python already has several libraries and tools that you are able to create automated tests for the application.

Integration Tests and Unit Tests

The world of testing is going to come with a lot of terminologies, and now that you know the difference between manual and automated testing. Now it is time to go a little bit deeper. Think of how you might test the lights that are on your car. You would first turn on the lights, which is your test step. And then you would go out of the car or ask a friend to check whether the lights turned on. This is going to be known as the test assertion. Testing more than one component here is going to be known as integration testing.

Think about all of the things that you would like to have worked correctly just to get a simple task the right results that you are looking for. These components are like the parts that come with your application, all of the modules, the functions, and the classes.

A big challenge that comes with this kind of testing is going to show up when the test doesn't give you the results that you would like. It can be hard for you to figure out what the issue is if you are not able to isolate the part of the system that isn't doing the work that you want. If the lights don't turn on in the car, what could be the problem? Is it the battery dying, the bulbs being broken, the computer of the car failing or something else?

If you have a newer car, it is possible that it is going to be able to tell you what is going on. And it is able to do this with the help of a unit test. The unit test is going to be a smaller test, one that is able to check that a single component is operating in the way that it should. It is the best way to isolate what is broken in the application, and then you can go right there and get it fixed.

Both the integration test and the unit test are things that you are able to work on inside of Python. To be able to write this kind of unit test to check out the built-in function sum(), you would need to check out the output of sum() against the output that you know needs to come out.

As you can see, there are a lot of different reasons why you will want to work with testing in Python. It will ensure that you are able to get the best results with your work, and can make it easier to debug the system and get it to work the way that you would like. Check out some of the things that we just talked about in this guidebook and this chapter, and see how easy it can be to test out some of your codes.

Chapter 13: What are the Regular Expressions in This Coding Language

Regular expressions are another fun thing that you will get to enjoy when it is time to work on the Python coding language. When you first get started with this language, take some time to see what is found in the library. You may be amazed at all that is there inside of it. This library is going to have a lot of regular expressions, ones that are going to help you do the searches that are needed to make your code work behind the scenes

These expressions are something that you will use in your coding because it will filter out all of the different kinds of texts that you have. it is possible to check and then see whether a string or some other text is going to be present in your code, and then see if it matches back up to the regular expression as well. And when you work with these kinds of expressions, you will find that the syntax is going to be the same each time, which makes it a bit easier to keep track of and remember. Learning how to do this on Python, and you will find that you can use it with some other coding languages as well.

Now that we have taken a look at these regular expressions a bit, you may need a definition to go with them so that you ensure they are used properly when it is time to bring them out. a good place to start with this is to open up your text editor, and then see if you are able to locate a word that has been spelled in two different ways in the same code. We will look through some of the steps to take to make this happen and to ensure that all of the confusion that comes with regular expressions so that you can handle this and any other problems that may come up when you are working with regular expressions.

You will find that working with regular expressions can be a lot of fun because they will open up a world of things that you are now able to do with your code. This is why it is so important for you to learn the right way for you to use them. Any time that you are ready to start adding these to your code, the first thing to do is import the expression library. You are able to use this when the program is first started up because it is something that you will use often.

As you work on your codes in Python, you will notice that regular expressions are going to start showing up on a regular basis. And if you are able to learn how to make these works, you will then be able to see some new things happen in your code as well. Now that we know a bit more about these regular expressions, let's take it a bit further and figure out how to use these to get the results that we are looking for.

The basic patterns to look for

There are a lot of things to pay attention to when you start to bring out those regular expressions. This is because there are a lot of choices that these regular expressions are going to be able to help you out with. One of the nice things about them though is that you aren't just going to bring them out with fixed characters all of the time. you can also use them to help you watch out for a few patterns when needed. A few of the most common patterns that come to play when we use regular expressions in the Python code will include

1. , X, 9, < -- ordinary characters just match themselves exactly. The meta-characters that aren't going to match themselves simply because they have a special meaning include: . ^ $ * ? { [] and more.
2. . (the period)—this is going to match any single except the new line symbol of '\n'
3. 3. \w—this is the lowercase w that is going to match the "word" character. This can be a letter, a digit, or an underbar. Keep in mind that this is the mnemonic and

that it is going to match a single word character rather than the whole word.

4. \b—this is the boundary between a non-word and a word.

5. \s—this is going to match a single white space character including the form, form, tab, return, newline, and even space. If you do \S, you are talking about any character that is not a white space.

6. ^ = start, $ = end—these are going to match to the end or the start of your string.

7. \t, \n, \r—these are going to stand for tab, newline, and return

8. \d—this is the decimal digit for all numbers between 0 and 9. Some of the older regex utilities will not support this so be careful when using it

9. \ --this is going to inhibit how special the character is. If you use this if you are uncertain about whether the character has some special meaning or not to ensure that it is treated just like another character.

Of course, these are just a few of the different regular expressions that you will be able to use when you get started in the Python coding language. But they are the ones that are the most important, and the ones that you should learn early on, so make sure to practice them a bit in your codes and on your compiler, to ensure that you are going to get the best results with them possible.

Doing your own queries with regular expressions

In addition to a few of the basic patterns that you will be able to look for in code, like what we showed above, you are able to take some of the regular expressions and use them to complete a search. This search can be done on any input string that is found in your code. There are actually three methods that you are able to use, and as you will see in a moment, there are some definite times when you will decide to use each one. Each time that you use a program, you may find that you need to re-evaluate which type of query is going to work the way that you want. You will find a use for each one; you just need to make sure that you are pulling them up at the right time. You will discover the different queries that you are able to do when you are on this program when you work with Python and regular expressions.

The search method

The first query type that you are able to do with the regular expressions that you have is going to be the search method.

This one is a great place to start because you are able to do your query and see if it matches up with any part of the code. The function isn't going to come with restrictions like you will find with some of the others we will look at. If you would like an opportunity to look through the entirety of the string, rather than looking at the beginning, or at the end, then this search method is going to help you get that done.

This search method is going to make it so that a programmer, or a user, is able to go through and look for something, no matter where it may be present inside of the string. Whether the term is in the beginning, at the end, or somewhere in between, you will be able to use the search method to help you find what you want. The syntax that you will need to use in order to bring out the hat search method will include:

```
import re
string = 'apple, orange, mango, orange'
match = re.search(r'orange', string)
print(match.group(0))
```

Before we go any further, it is time to take a moment and add this above syntax into your compiler and see what results you are going to get. For this one in particular, if you did it the proper way, then your output is going to be the word "orange." With this method, you will only see it match up once, regardless of how many times the word of orange ends up showing itself in the string. There could be one orange or twenty oranges; you will get the same output with this one. Once the program has been able to find the first orange, assuming that any string you design is going to have that word in it, then it will stop.

The match method

Now that we have had a chance to work with the search method, it is time to move on to another method that you can focus on. The search method is able to help you in some cases, but there are also going to be times when it is not going to be just right for the code that you want to write out. the match method is going to find the matches to your query, but the location is going to be important. It is only going to pull up the output when your query is right at the beginning of the string. It is going to be responsible for looking out for a specific pattern inside the syntax that you are looking for.

Let's take a look at the example that we did above. You will see that there is going to be a pattern there. This is that the word of orange is going to be between the other words. But when you do the query of re_match, rather than the re_search that we did before, then you aren't going to get a result. This is because the word of orange is not the first one on the list.

Even though you do have the object of orange showing up in the code (and in this case, it is showing up more than once), you are not going to see it show up. This is simply because that word is not the first one in the string. In the case that we are looking at, you find that the word apple is the first one. With this match method, it is only going to do a query of the first word, and if that doesn't match up with what you want, then there is no output.

If you end up having a pattern that is not in the right order when you start out with this, then you won't be able to get the right answers that you want until you change things around. You can change it around while writing the code, but once the code is running, you can't go back through in the middle of the program and make the changes. So, when you are writing out the code, double check that the words end up in the right places along the way.

When you are ready to work with the match method, and you want to see how it works, just take the syntax that we worked on earlier with the search method, but switch out the re_search part with re_match. This is all that you will need to do in order to make this all work the way that you would like.

The findall method

 There are also times when you want to be able to find out how many of a particular object is in your string. If you go with the other methods, you will just find out whether the object is the first in the pattern or if there is that object in the string at all. But with the findall method, you will be able to find all of the oranges that are in the string. Using the example above, the findall method would provide you with the output of "orange, orange" since there are two of them present there.

You can have as many of the same object in your string as you would like, or you can pick out any other object as well. If you added ten more oranges in there, the findall method would list out orange ten times. If you wanted to find out how many apples are there, you could use the findall method and in this example, only get apple to show up once.

To see how the findall method will work differently than the search method we discussed before, take a moment and experiment. Bring up your compiler and use the code that we had in the search method. Replace the search part with findall and see what happens.

Then go through and mess around with the list a little bit. Take things away, add more objects, and play around to see what will happen to your output each time that you do this. This is a good way to practice your regular expressions and you can even throw in the match method to learn better how each of these works.

Do I need to use those square brackets?

Before we end this chapter, it is time to take a look at some of the proper coding rules that can make your life easier. As you are writing a lot of the codes that are found in this language, you may find that some square brackets are going to show up in the codes that you are reading. These are going to make it easier to indicate a specific set of characters and will ensure that those are going to be kept apart from the other ones.

A good example is when you would like to write out a statement. You may write it out as [abc], you will then be able to get a match back for a, b, or c. This is going to make it easier because then you are able to get the matches back for them rather than having to do individual searches on each part.

There are other types of characters, such as working with the \w and\s will work with these kinds of square brackets as well, and you want to make sure that these are used. The only exception that comes with this rule is that the dot is just a dot, and you aren't able to go through and match up these, even if you find that they are already in the square brackets from before.

The example that we already went through and did before is a great way to show you what you can do with the regular expressions if you need to add them into your code, and you will need to make sure that you know how to use them to get the results that you would like. There is so much that you are able to do when you work on these regular expressions, and they can come into play, even with some of the more difficult parts of the code that you are trying to work with.

To help you with this a bit more, and to make sure that you have the regular expressions down, it is time to practice a few with your interpreter. Try out some of the examples and mess around with them a bit, seeing how they work and what little adjustments are going to do to the code as a whole.

Conclusion

Thank for making it through to the end of *Python for beginners*, let's hope it was informative and able to provide you with all of the tools you need to achieve your goals whatever they may be.

The next step is to start writing out some of your own codes with the help of the Python coding language. There is so much to love about this coding language, and both beginners and those who have been coding for a long time, and this is why this kind of language has such a following and a community throughout the world.

This guidebook has taken some time to look at the different things that you are able to do when it comes to working with the Python code. From the conditional statements, the loops, working with exceptions, and more, you will soon be on the trail to writing some of your own codes in no time at all.

When you are ready to learn a bit more about working with the Python code and all of the cool things that you are able to do with this kind of coding language, regardless of how much experience you have with technology and coding in the past, make sure to check out this guidebook to help you get started.

Finally, if you found this book useful in any way, a review on Amazon is always appreciated!

www.ingramcontent.com/pod-product-compliance
Lightning Source LLC
Chambersburg PA
CBHW070232180526
45158CB00001BA/430